Grace
Note
Peter Godfrey

STACK
BOOKS

Smokestack Books
1 Lake Terrace, Grewelthorpe, Ripon HG4 3BU
e-mail: info@smokestack-books.co.uk
www.smokestack-books.co.uk

ISBN 9781739772208

Smokestack Books
is represented by
Inpress Ltd

Remembering
Wênita Pereira
Gomes de Lima

With thanks

Some of these poems first appeared in the *Morning Star, Northwords Now, Never Bury Poetry*, and in the following collections: *A Kist of Thistles: An anthology of radical poetry from contemporary Scotland, Handbook for 2021: The Bread & Roses Poetry Award Anthology 2020*, and *The Cry of the Poor: An anthology of radical writing about poverty*, all published by Culture Matters.

I would like to record my gratitude to a series of gifted writing tutors: the late Julia Casterton, Christina Dunhill, the redoubtable Mimi Khalvati, Gillian Clarke and Pauline Prior-Pitt, who illuminated some of the mysteries of poetry.

Contents

Carioca girl

Sometimes I feel
I'm still on a bus in Rio de Janeiro
careering down the road.

The night is charged and torrid
and we're pushed close, clinging to the hand-rail,
swaying with the movement of the crowd.

You smile, and we get talking –
the sea behind me,
lights left trailing in the dark.

With every bend a surge
of sweating bodies; at each bump
people lurch, squeezed tight and laughing.

The driver brakes – a dust cloud, Ipanema.
Soon we'll get off together
at the next stop.

Recife café

Reading of bombs and wars
I set eyes on Thaciane,

offered her the half a bag
of cashew nuts that I had left

and what a smile!
Did she have a home?

The street. A family?
Yes, far off in the *interior*

where they grew manioc
and she used to go to school.

Now she helped her aunt
to gather drink cans,

sell them for recycling,
and slept beneath the city's bridges.

I delved into
the comfort of my pocket,

watched how she warmed to
just two *reals* of care –

gangling, barefoot,
fair shock of sun-bleached hair,

the shadow of
a white tooth in her smile.

Red Bishop

'When I give food to the poor, they call me a saint. When I ask why the poor have no food, they call me a Communist.'
Dom Helder Câmara

Here in the cathedral at Olinda
though your voice is gone
a breeze ruffles fresh flowers,
the church bell tolls,
a single bird in flight
carries your *credo*
out through palm trees
over the turquoise sea,
the sole, heretical truth –
I've seen the beggars
and the glue-sniffing boys –
that food and shelter
are for all to share,
a baby's cry is
holier than angels.

The Labour Exchange, Bobigny

You board the Métro at Jacques Bonsergent – line 5
then surface at the terminus, strike out
across the eerie bus station, hop on
a slim blue tram for Seine-Saint-Denis.

Tower blocks crowd a cloudless August sky,
relieved by just one tree, and you are squashed
with people from all parts, their weighty bags,
are told: 'Alight one stop past Libération.'

It rises like a crest in wavy concrete
from the flagstones, half-submerged, a ship of state.
Above, two men survey a sea of pavement,
spread their cardboard beds, bask in the sun.

The entrance is a secret down a slipway –
you step through wide glass doors, are welcome here.
Curved walls invite you along sinuous corridors
that have no edges, seem to have no end,

open on meeting-rooms starry with lights,
low-ceilinged, confidential, where a lie
would wash up naked and a pose be punctured
by guffaws. Here talk is comradely, forthright.

A scalloped theatre greets you, unsuspected,
flowing blue and yellow walls, ocean and beach,
plush proletarian seats – Niemeyer's swirling claim
the poor Paris *banlieue* could be Copacabana.

On your bike

The glory of pedalling the wrong
way on a one-way street,
for now the order of the world is
this: black will be white
and monarchs road-sweepers.

Taking corners like the Manx TT,
knees grazing the pavement,
we breeze through red
that might as well be green,
past cars in a smoky veil.

A policeman's on his beat as I
wheel by market porters
with their blood-smeared aprons
on this hillock, once a gallows –
here Wat Tyler harangued the king.

The moon glimpsed in a wedge of sky,
I whirl down Pudding Lane,
the FT Index up, it's 12.04, 18 degrees –
so what, I'm an angel fish
in a school of rainbow stripes.

Paris '69

With an armful of baguettes too hot to hold
I trailed behind the *patron* through Les Halles –
green wrought-iron canopies, outside still dark.
He probed some fruit, arrayed and plentiful

then we made for the hotel: a metal vat
of steaming coffee grounds and chicory
that I ladled into bowls, served guests
who wandered down in dribs and drabs,

materialised from crannies, came in seasick
off the rickety staircase to *pain croustillant*,
hushed conversations, while the English night porter,
moustachioed, stopped reading *Fanny Hill*

and took the Métro home. 'You really need
a uniform,' the *patron* mused. In cold mid-morning
we set out again to Prisunic, his thin grey hair
slicked back: he was wizened, small,

dreamt of a box at L'Opéra, of *cent mille balles*.
He rummaged for a charcoal polyester smock
that buttoned at the shoulder – more dentist than *garçon* –
said *that* would befit Le Grand Hôtel du Globe.

In the makeshift lounge squeezed on the mezzanine
and bathed by orange light I swapped thoughts
with two postgrads from the USA who had a baby,
discovered visions shared could span the ocean.

Impromptu soirées fired those gathered there –
spellbound by fellowship we spoke of what could be,
breathed air still busy with revolt, ideas cascading
down the stairwell, talk brimful of possibility,

our anthems on the turntable, new 45s:
Nicole Croisille, Aufray and Polnareff –
the tunes that sent our spirits soaring
and belied the grave, dour admonitions of De Gaulle.

Banter in the white-tiled kitchen, a *rosbif*
with Jean in his tall chef's hat, half a finger severed,
broad vowels of *Le Midi*, with Ali the wry *plongeur*
and Jacqueline the waitress, lovestruck in another part of town;

Philippe the *commis* chef riding in on his *Solex*
with winklepickers and a quiff, telling me
of home in Alsace, where later I'd visit him,
turn up a rusted helmet on the hillside near Verdun;

chance midnight rendezvous with fashion students
from London – I chatted to a chic, slim girl,
beguiled by long blond hair. *Vin rouge* stained our smiles,
but any more I was too awed to dare.

Striking out over the cobbles of Pont-Neuf,
tripping up by a red-lit dive in steep Pigalle,
catching my second matinee of the new Buñuel
while workers marched on streets shiny with rain...

Between the Louvre and plate glass of Palais Royal
a story opened at a run-down hostelry
tucked in a backwater, Le Grand Hôtel du Globe –
dingy, compelling, where a rebel cowed leapt free.

Ricardo

¡Fui un malillo! I was a rogue
and loved the girls to bits,
then left them behind like fish-bones.
Look at me now – 78 and wheezing.
I never married. *Soy soltero.*
Just to catch my breath
is sweet as any kiss.

But to see the almond blossom
in February clinging to the hillside
gives some recompense.
These terraces with their aquifers
hewn by the Moors into steep slopes
still hold good. My pick too
turned the thin Andalusian soil.

It must have been... 1932 when
I heard Lorca address a rally in Órgiva.
War found me on the factory floor
assembling munitions for the republic,
but the village went with Franco. Returning,
I was shunned by those from
the Falangist trenches. They still look away.

University was a dream to me, but then
what nature doesn't give you
Salamanca can't bestow!
I bathed myself in books – astronomy
brought the stars inside my window –
warming my feet by the *brasero* under the table,
on it my inhaler and a glass of red wine.

Often I feel like a leveret
on the snow-line sitting here in
the whitewashed house where I was born.
Each afternoon, when the bus winds its way
from Granada, I don my trilby
and walk haltingly down to the square
to fetch the newspaper my brother sends me.

The Married Priest

'As for the mystery and enigma in my paintings, I would say that it is the best proof of my break with the set of absurd mental habits that generally take the place of an authentic feeling of existence.'
René Magritte

It's raining stockbrokers.
Yesterday it was lemons,
tomorrow it may be prayers
but let's not speculate.
All the evidence is of
bowler-hats clanking
on curtained windows
as pinstriped men intimidate
traffic, confront the police
with their heinous deeds
before disappearing down
grey gutters, gurgling and
doffing their hats as they go.

*

I'll buy you diamonds
or maybe a kilo of pears
to wrap around your charabanc
whenever the train's not on time.
Where clouds are edifices
tied with a rope of waves,
the galleon of November
has dreamt us away with its dawn.

*

The crime of the pope
was to fry oysters at 30,000 feet,
to yodel in a blackbird's gentle twitter.
The crime of the pope was
to waddle into oblivion on a shoestring
and still want to keep the change
from a footballer's knee.

*

All's quiet in the village. I wish
the moon would stop scratching my neck.
It's been blowing a gale for a fortnight –
sleep comes when you put out the snail.

*

Steepling into the forest –
clip-clop, clip-clop.
A 10–1 chance on good fortune,
jovial as hunchback prawns.
Where days are flat as antelopes
with the aplomb of bandaged tom-toms,
nubile as a landlord
you may treat with the foliage of bones.
Rider, you go!

Once in Aragón

'It never rains in August
so it was then
we had the monastery roof repaired.

The workmen put up scaffolding,
took their time,
then – I still don't believe it –

wind blew from the dry Monegros,
sand swept in
and the night of August 25th

a violent thunderstorm broke.
The monks ran up to pull tarpaulins,
blankets over the octagonal chapel

but rain fell down the walls in torrents
and all but ruined
the frescoes by Ramón Bayeu.

We'd prayed and we were helpless.'
The father confessor smiled –
he may have shrugged.

All that love: the minute brush-strokes,
figures with gilded haloes,
pink and blue pastel shades

smudged,
smoothed over,
and the walls that cried.

Patagonia

Her grandfather came on an immigrant ship –
the *Rebecca* sailed from Liverpool non-stop,
bedraggled, with a necklace of hawsers and hope.
There were indians then, but one by one
they died of the common cold. The landscape,
too vast to remind him of Capel Curig,
was just as wild and thrilling on the breath.

'That chapel with the rusting iron roof lying
squat along the valley of Chubut is where
he used to preach. We've an *eisteddfod* now –
you may meet our new bard, Don Luis Enrique
Jones. Still I find it strange shopping on
Calle Berwyn Williams, greeting friends
somewhere between *Buenos días* and *Bore da.'*

Up the coast are sea-lions, groaning manatees
and inland by the Scottish farmstead
is a broad lake daubed pink with flamingos.
Rawson, Puerto Madryn – names to make even
a Welsh woman bow her head – where Admiral Massera,
prince of torture, refined his taste in the long years
of the boot. 'These are my bearings.'

The Horgabost Bard

They razed the township to the ground
and folk fled to the east.
'Let them live on rock!' – the bays
with only fish and peat

while the *machair* and its lazy-beds
the cottar dug dead true
were turned to pasture for the sheep
where a blaze of spring flowers grew.

My ancestors built shielings in the lee
of gales that swept the Minch,
huddled to fend off the tacksman, goitre
and famine, chanting hymns

that spilled out on the sabbath by the creels
of Manish, of Lingerabay
and Geocrab where I went to school
and tweed was waulked and swathed.

Some set sail for Cape Breton
or fought the empire's wars.
The laird and his ghillies rode for deer
and lichen stained my toes.

But it was only in the '30s
we could come back west –
the open sky and long white strand,
ball of fire that set

beyond the mirage of St. Kilda,
painting the green sea rose.
Orchids bloomed in the dunes for me,
the waymark MacLeod's Stone.

My brother worked on a merchantman
but you'll find me at the fank
or on the croft turning vegetables,
a *Hearach* in his land.

Our three girls are away now. We've
a home that has been blessed
with a warm hearth and the skirl of pipes –
no better warp and weft.

There's a threnody in Gaelic song
that recounts my forebears' plight.
Do draw your chair up to the stove –
I'll sing it for you one night.

Staying over

'You take the child's room.'
And I did,
a door away from her, a breath –

and the door ajar:
I could almost hear her breath
on the secret pillow.

'I might let you in,' she didn't say,
hung gentle
in the night-time tremor.

I sat amid
the complicity of whispers,
dark dome of silence

where 3 o'clock is mauve,
lamplight a travesty,
edging the small bed –

then lay back
under the laughing lion bedspread,
settled for sleep.

Breakfast
was a wholesome affair,
friendly as cereals.

Hostelling

for Katrin and Jeremy

She brings gladioli, armfuls,
and sunflowers from the garden.
Fragrant pink lilies stop you on the stairs.

The window-sill is fragile with anemones –
red, blue, translucent. A nasturtium's
orange flame tangles with green.

Scones and rolls are heaped up
on the table – fare left over from
his brother's restaurant – storage jars of jam:

damson cooling he made the night before,
raspberry, strawberry for breakfast,
marmalades from different years.

Boots and rucksacks by the door
we savour the day, offerings
of cereals and fresh-ground coffee,

gather round to share the feast laid
in the cramped kitchen
of their hostel, their home.

Ferry to Skye

We glide so stealthily
      from moorings
         to a lustrous sea
           where cliffs are cut-outs,
                islands beads,
                    towards a slow horizon.
            Trawlers plough
         white furrows,
     clouds like waistcoats
    cling to rugged
leftovers of land.

On Whalsay

Waves a-tumble
like tresses of your hair.
Fetlar in mist across the sea.
A diadem of hope compressed to stone.

Rhenigidale

Soft, primeval,
water trickling down a stream,

                beating of a gull's wings
                by the shingle,

the wind walking
in short steps,

                sky unfurling
                over fingered rocks

as if held up
by fabled columns,

                while pink thrift quivers
                on salt leaves

and grass ruffles
the shirtsleeves of a wave.

His statue by the shore

'Do you know where I'd find firelighters?'
I showed him, earned his peering gratitude.

I made out, flustered, not to recognise him –
George, the boyish, square-jawed man

with wild grey hair and hollow cheeks.
We went the way of our respective baskets.

Later he was walking down the hill
carrying two plastic bags back into town.

I longed to join him, knew paths don't cross twice
by chance – but held back, shy to break his step

and viewed him – some rare bird,
the real Mackay – across the road.

I'd seen him on the sea-front years before,
imagined him as always there,

as much of Stromness as the ferry sliding into port
or flagstones winding under Brinkie's Brae.

A man who'd anchored on his island,
savoured every *haar* and voe,

drawn words like baked scones from the oven,
Brown, in the kitchen of his council house –

that frail man with the modest face
I'd never thought was stone.

Betty Corrigall's grave

Betty from Greengairs Cottage
on the shores of Rysa Bay,
did your love go to the whaling,
for the *nor'wast* sail away?

You'd seen the hare up Trowieglen
vanish white against the snow.
By lochans you picked blaeberries,
made the rounded hills your own.

You found that you were left with child,
dark-haired girl who hadn't wed,
and walked your shame into the sea –
they hauled you from the dead.

You sobbed your grief into a byre,
flung a rope over a beam,
the din of hellfire in your ears,
no kinsfolk to be seen.

They'd not bury you in hallowed ground
to mourn your sailor boy.
You were cast out to the border –
neither Melsetter nor Hoy.

On a bleak peat moor they laid you down,
torn away from home,
bog and bracken for your bed,
green moss, shunned and alone.

I stand in shifts of rain, in wind
too hard to catch my breath,
by the island's crags and crevices
amid hailstones, ferns and heather.

Away from land the ocean's turquoise,
frantic with spindrift lace.
Betty, you'd know how my heart sang
when I made out a far ship's wake.

Annie Morrison's hat

My father wore it just before he died –
we rowed out to spot seals off Blakeney Point.
It's been with me in Pyrenean ice,
on Biscay and where southern oceans join.

You were the best known knitter in the isles
and told me over tea and girdle scones
of girlhood spent barefoot walking in gales
when only candles flickered, lanterns shone.

You wove warm strands of Hebridean wool –
your last years saw our strand of friendship forged.
How often I've mislaid it, felt a fool
till someone comes up: 'Is this blue hat yours?'

and I retrieve that fabric of the few.
I know the benediction comes from you.

His Master's Voice

Rust carpet rough against my knees
on the living-room floor
as I conjured crackly voices, dance bands
through the plaited fascia
of the smooth teak gramophone:

Horseguards on Parade in Whitehall
pacing there before me,
Coronation Scot whooshing past
and sooting up the window,
The Laughing Policeman tirelessly splitting his sides.

For my parents it was musicals: *Annie Get Your Gun*
('Anything you can do I can do better'),
or Peggy Lee singing *Tenderly* –
I just couldn't hear the tune,
but since learned every generation has to smooch.

Discs in paper sleeves that were my fellowship
kept by my parents strapped in laundry cases,
their labels navy, black, maroon
quite sober till they'd start to spin
caressed by the secret diamond needle.

But occasionally a record would get stuck,
the arm slewed right across it
like some wayward sailor,
or one of the stack of 78s would crack as it fell
then split off into an evil crescent moon

and I'd go running
into the kitchen, petrified
('I can do anything better than you'),
knowing that there was no one
to mend my carousel of dreams.

Collector's item

I swapped you a stamp
from the Comoros Islands,
Turks & Caicos, the Maldives,

went gathering cocoa
on the Gold Coast,
climbed the mountains of Nyasaland.

I touched the fez of the Persian shah,
could almost decode the script
of the orange children of Formosa.

One day kind Mr. Leaman
in his trilby gave me
the biggest stamp I'd ever seen

on a letter someone sent him
from Colombia, with a president
who meant nothing to me.

I got home elated,
soaked it for my album
then found the perforation torn.

There were sorties to
Aden, Ceylon,
the Dutch East Indies.

But what I really wanted
was the £1 deep carmine
from *Kenya, Uganda and Tanganyika*

with flamingos on the lake
flanking a gold medallion
of King George.

It was so rare
you said that you'd swap me
the ten-shilling one

in pale cornflower blue,
the king's head
a drop of wine.

On the round

I heard the horse come clopping down the road,
leapt out of bed and dressed, ran to help out –

the blinkered chestnut rummaged in its nosebag
while Roy unloaded crates from off the cart.

'A pint of red-top there at number 9,
one silver opposite for Mrs Lynch,'

while he took four, five bottles in each hand
like skittles wedged between his chunky fingers

and strode across the kerb from door to door
collecting empties, reading scribbled notes.

I clutched the milk, delivered it with care –
what if I dropped it? But I didn't, didn't.

Roy jotted details in his leather book
that seemed to be the bible, slammed it closed

then shook the reins – a snort and we were off
up Brent Street, Egerton Gardens, down Queens Road

though it was only dawn, neighbours asleep –
I liked to be with this kind, swarthy man,

his black hair brylcreemed back, stud in his ear –
a gypsy, some said, from a foreign land.

'One sterilized for 10b' – curtains drawn
on sickness, age. 'You know the Kemps have gold?'

And how I did, the yellow cream set thick –
they must be wealthy: others had silver and red.

I hopped off by the park to go to school,
but two pints in one hand I never dared.

Roy took a fourpenny orange from the crate,
gave it to me with a calloused pat

and smile, or if he'd heard my silent plea
opened the hallowed cold store and pulled out

a bottle of chocolate milk fresh from the dairy.
I tore off, fumbled open my sixpence-worth

and almost downed it in one draught
gulping the morning, gladdest boy on earth.

The Fish

Cloud washing the sky,
a slate-grey sea
beneath our wooden boat.

Twang of the line tautening –
he reeled it in
and at the end wriggled

a flat fish,
brown, submerged,
wanting to return

to a hidden world.
His tentative hands
unhooked its wounded lip

and left it flapping
on the boards
with its two skewed eyes.

The wind was getting up now
so he rowed for shore.
I see-sawed to the waves.

With rolled up trousers
and stone jerkin
he waded onto the beach

and hauled the boat in
over a ruckus of pebbles,
the fish's gills gasping for brine.

He grabbed some driftwood,
dashed it on the head,
his face wrinkled with distaste,

stilling its gorgeous orange freckles –
the kindest thing, he said
to end its misery.

It was the last time
my father went fishing,
the last time I was a child.

Not watching *55 Days in Peking*

Side by side
in the dark cinema,

her lacquered blond hair
crisp against my hand

as my arm slipped furtive as a snake
along the backrest.

The sudden warm breath –
someone else's,

smear of lips and longing
and the hidden realm of tongues.

Together in crushed velvet seats
beyond the usherette's dim torch,

our hands pretending
not to know each other.

And when the lights came up,
too shy to look straight at you

but the world had changed –
bond of saliva, lipstick proud.

Space race

for the Talimonovs

Astronauts and cosmonauts
whirling round the sun,
docking with their space stations
like felons on the run
                    – the Earth looks tiny.

Astronauts and cosmonauts
weightless as a cloud –
your sputniks and your satellites
will do your patrons proud
                    – and you like bubbles.

Astronauts and cosmonauts,
is it really blue,
this world where we tread lightly
that still has its pull on you?
                    You'd hardly notice.

Is there life on Venus,
are there men on Mars?
Can you see holes in outer space,
our future in the stars?
                    I wish you'd tell us.

Give my love to Khruschev,
Kennedy and Ike.
Fly the hammer and sickle,
plant the stars and stripes
                    – it's only human.

And when you come back down to Earth,
your feet are on the ground,
will you greet your comrades
or invite your buddies round?
                    Mind the iron curtain.

Do you fear the red menace?
Are you sick of Uncle Sam?
Astronauts and cosmonauts,
could the cold war be a sham?
                    Let's have a good laugh and shake hands.

December roses

The Christmas vac –
most students had gone home.
She came sweeping through the courtyard
in her russet dress,
slightly huddled from the cold.

The girl I'd seen on stage
and I knew vaguely,
who'd had a boyfriend here –
an emissary
from forbidden Girton.

Would she come up for coffee?
She said yes!
We shared the sofa in my college room –
the term was threadbare
and the year was running down.

I'd dared not dream of this –
her look intent
and searching, gilded fire,
long chestnut hair that grazed
a twist of pain playing in her smile.

We kissed – perhaps she pressed
against me... pull and tow
of things lived and what's yet to be –
some crossroads, Elysian way.
Was it for me?

In the post

'Did you get my card?'
The one I was thirsting for,
all the way from Spain.
It never arrived, so
I planned summer without you.

*

'I wrote you a long letter
in response to yours.'
Maybe the village postman
in the Pyrenees
didn't hand it on.

They say that in his attic there's a stash.
White-haired and smoking
at the wheel of his estate,
his small eyes dart,
won't look me in the face.

Mine had been
a love letter of sorts.
Feeling like a monk, wanting
to share the rhythms
of the harvest with you,

the shy peak of *el Aspe*
rough at the head of the valley,
its dark rock patched with snow,
sun dappling the poplars
and steep light green fields.

*

Tucked in my parents' bureau
an orange stick of sealing wax
melted with black
lay next to vellum paper,
deckle-edged.

Folded wishes slipped
in an envelope, reflections
pressed down with saliva,
a secret launched
across the world...

What if the stamp peeled off,
someone took a shine to it
at a sorting office in Argentina?
The letter may have crumpled
in some mailbag with its furrowed brow.

Perhaps the address smudged in the rain,
a loose corner flap turned up
and it unravelled. Or it took a wrong turning,
ended up wedged between
the postmaster's floorboards in Ladakh.

*

One morning a brightly coloured card
drifts through the letter box,
a piece of breath, impassioned scribble,
settles like a butterfly
on the mat.

John Raymond Roberts, RN

'*Bechgyn bochgoch ar aelwydydd*
gloyw, yn heidio i dir estron.'
(*'Rose-cheeked lads from cheery hearths*
herded off to foreign lands.')
Menna Elfyn

At school in Llanrug he used to go
with the girls to cookery classes. If he was home
he'd always make a pie or something –

he'd do nice things: eclairs, or shortbread,
his favourite. It was the careers teacher
who said the best place for young cooks was

the Navy – to be a chef and sail the seven seas.
He joined up at sixteen. The last letter we had
was from Ascension Island: *Feeling fine* –

I'm getting lovely and brown. It's an
awful lot colder down by South Georgia –
you couldn't live long in the water there.

(One winter when they were kids
here in Llanberis they came to the door
like statues, frozen stiff from playing

on the sledge. They were four musketeers
together by the slate quarry or on the slopes
of Snowdon – his sister's never been the same.)

San Carlos Bay – what a death trap, the entrance
so narrow they had nowhere to run. Like the *Antelope*,
Sir Galahad, just a sitting duck for that bomb.

They were dishing out sandwiches on deck when
it happened, the electrics all off. He volunteered
to firefight – they were burning, weren't they?

If there'd been a Sea Wolf missile system
on board the *Ardent* it may well have
saved them. The Admiralty reckoned it too dear.

A friend of his from Conwy has been bad
ever since returning. His cousin flew out recently –
he says there's more on Anglesey than there.

Capel Coch was overflowing for the service
in his memory. Months later we'd still hear
the thud of his case as he came home on leave.

La Quinta del Sordo

after Goya

In the Deaf Man's House
there's the drunk sound of a mandolin,
two witches sup from a bowl of gruel,

the goat of darkness speaks
before a hundred shifting eyes
and fauns drift over fields of battle.

Hags wind up hills on pilgrimages
and the fat-lipped penitent
in black, all black, astounded

by the devil's guise, beats out
the chorus of a drowned man's hymn
while cowhands club each other senseless.

La Mezquita

I walked through keyhole arches: cream, vermilion
and to my left more trees of stone were rising –
if there was one there may have been a million.

A forest of pillars on my right was hiding
more exquisite arches: vermilion, cream,
carved foliage on their capitals and gliding

skywards like some never-ending dream
or image of forever, harmonious
peace of Moors, Christians and Sephardim –

al-Andalus's people: no erroneous
hates or bigotry, or reason of the sword
but an enlightened moment, glorious

and predicated on the open word,
informed by Arab grammar, geometry –
not a war hero but learning was *their* lord.

In the Alhambra's shallow pool you could see
an image of the cupola so high
and plunge through reflections into infinity.

This poise and equilibrium bathed in time
was smashed by the iron-spiked inquisitor
who'd countenance no other, vilify

the Jewess with *'Ave María'* above her door,
Abdul who'd thought to change his name to Juan,
garrotte them, or banish them to foreign shores.

Among the chiselled fronds I had begun
to hear the muezzin's wail, the caliph's prayer –
or was it the gypsy singer sick with love,

staunch as a Roman buttress on the Guadalquivir
and fording the river on its well set course
with plangent cries for her no longer here

where farmers, shepherds too harnessed the force
of passing currents, made their order?
Listen! The clop of the hooves of Lorca's horse
through the cobbled alleys of Córdoba.

Skirmishes

She was the girl on the deck with a tear in her jeans
aboard the ferry to the mainland from the island of Coll.
My binoculars scanned the suggestion of hills through the mist,
raindrops stinging my cheeks in my anorak hood.
She was travelling solo, memories buckled in her bag.
My focus came closer to shearwaters in the white spray.
The yearning to talk to her swept like a squall up the firth.

A voice soaring over mountains, hair jet as the Mapuche,
high-cheekboned, guitar glinting, of her place. She told
of the south: *araucaria* trees, beads of islands threading
down to the strait. I too learned to sing of the Andes,
of a ribbon of land torn and choked with lament. Tunes by
Victor, Violeta were a torrent in her eyes – we melted
the statues of Europe, but our song remained inside.

I met her in Cáceres station, bound for Madrid. Our walk
to the castellated walls took me clean by surprise, and
bedding down in an alcove we waited for the 3am train.
Her flat suffused with daylight, a book on Lenin by her bedside –
we dared to breathe adventure, but I'd a passage booked
the next night. All her grace, every sinew seemed to tell me
I could stay. If I had believed it as the ferry sailed away.

The Maya

When death takes me
I will follow, lay down
the *quetzal* feathers
of my plume. For skin is
the sketch, approximation
and glory a west wind
that slipped among
the *ceiba* trees one afternoon.

Meeting the *Wai-Wai*

Night held us in a pelt
of blackness – only a ferment
of chance beams swept
over features, silhouetted huts,
the smear of the Milky Way.

In the morning they brought
necklaces of seeds threaded
from the forest, bedecked me
with them, my yellow
hammock warm, swinging.

Beneath the straw *maloca*
we exchanged our *pão*
for their *beijú*, our *chā*
for their *bacaba*. Words in
halting tongues kindled the fire –

curious toddlers with dark fringes,
a sleeping, big-footed puppy.
Two hens scratched the earth
by the wooden manioc press.
Then we followed the jungle track

seven days' walk from Surinam
among high trees, mottled
fronds and creepers. A man whistled,
shot an old male monkey,
brought his booty home to skin.

Always time to dip in the sluicing river,
to sink a line for fish. I felt
the glow from those open faces,
a tiara of vermilion feathers
the *Wai-Wai* laid so lightly on my head.

Carrying it over

This journey's taken many years and
still the moon pours out its precious song.
I caught a glimpse of gold off Africa,
could swear I saw the shadow of contentment
as we crossed the strait.

Sometimes a smile may lead to
recondite stone dwellings in the mountains,
prise open creaking doors. At others
it gives onto a familiar land
where contours are the same. But

your next port of call may find you
sharp in appetite, astonished by bronze skin –
its smoothness, sheen – the wind
daredevil through your hair, and seashells
gems that tumble in your eyes.

Jacques Brel on tour in northern France

'La ville s'endormait –
j'en oublie le nom.'

November stubble in flat fields
that seem to stretch for ever
through a hotel window crying with rain
in a town I won't remember.

Low horizon a monotone
pierced by a church spire like a needle.
A desk, a lamp, a single bed,
my glass of *Orangina.*

I dip my nib into black ink,
scrawl words on flimsy paper –
a warm glow from my cigarette
but the groaning wind says 'never'.

Tonight I'll take the stage again,
belt songs into the darkness,
pressed tuxedo drenched with sweat,
tie loosed, collar unfastened.

I long for May and long for home,
a seagull blown inland.
Will I see you on streets clothed with fog
in Lille, Strasbourg, Verdun?

Oradour-sur-Glane, 10th June 1944

They reach out into the present –
naked chimneys, vacant doors,
the writhing iron where Jean-Baptiste
swung his hammer in the forge,

a rusted car with crumpled headlights,
the seized-up sewing-machine
in the draper's shop where Édith Leblanc
once quietly stitched a seam.

Never a *pastis* will be served
on green baize at *L'Estaminet*.
No hand on the cycle handlebars.
A tram line to who knows where?

Melted frieze of the church bell
with a tongue that couldn't toll.
Glasses from a vanished face.
Not a pen in the school inkwells.

Six hundred and forty-two people
flung into a heap.
Then the SS plundered the cellar
of the wine merchant, Jacques Denis,

got drunk on the finest vintages
and set the village ablaze,
the whispers of the rooftops,
a baby not yet named.

The Uist Boys

In the bitter wind of Ypres
two mates seek repose:
young MacPherson in his greatcoat,
slung rifle etched with snow

and, hands thrust deep in worsted,
on an icy wooden bench
Ewen Nicholson from Grimsay,
front line in the firing trench,

with his thin knees and glengarry hat,
wispy trace of tash and beard,
lips drawn tight, short of a smile,
as if seeing the end he fears.

They are cornered by their duty,
brass and khaki uniform,
made to gun down the marauding Boche.
Ewen sends a snapshot home

six days before his slaughter.
Now they share a Flanders grave –
lads who'd never live to savour
the press of an embrace.

Morag Ann

The peat fire scorched her legs in tartan
as wool slid between gnarled fingers.
She stitched an Aran knit she knew
by heart, yanked at a skein of navy yarn,
the curled up sheepdog regal on the rug.

Then she smoothed her handiwork –
it may win a rosette at the show
if she lived to see the summer through.
Who was it for? Not him. Three years,
D.A., without your wheezing breath.

The armchair empty where he'd sat upright,
a brown-stained forefinger traced
decades when he'd sailed the world
on Senior Service, Player's Weights.
He'd watch her in his oiled wool sweater,

whisper a word either side of silence.
An east wind wailed among the eaves.
Spit and crackle of peat thrown on the grate.
Faces in the flames. A Napoleon clock
over the beige-tiled fireplace ticked and tocked.

Kyleakin ferry remembered

Yellow crest – lion rampant
on a shiny red funnel
seen through mist and slanting rain,
smoke wafting with the wind.

Cars and lorries snug on deck
in a din of steel and rivets
that drifts out half a mile,
slips past its sister vessel.

Far-flung lamps a constellation,
green and red, dim white and blinking
as a searchlight arcs the cosmos,
falls on capstans and dark waves.

Hear the clank of chains
when the gangplank scrapes on concrete
and tousled knots of bladderwrack
flail, quiver, put to sea...

Now the ruined castle crumbles
in a hush of powdered drizzle.
Darkened cafés turn their backs –
no boat, no whisper on the pavement.

A crooked eyebrow spans the sound,
taunts the lighthouse, tides and eddies,
while voices carry on the breeze
from Kyle of Lochalsh.

MacDiarmid Hotel

I put in for the night
to MacDiarmid Hotel –
scratchy windows, bracken
around the doorposts.
A surly bell-boy made
room service slower than sleep.

A film of dust coated
the mantelpiece over
a tepid fire. There were beds
without springs and taps
that gushed, blundering fitfully
as you opened them.

Draughts blew through
cobwebbed alcoves. The silver
service had no lustre. Among
stained white table-cloths
a waif stirred breakfast:
a plate of gruel.

I never thought to pack
my bags. It would have
seemed churlish to lodge
a complaint with the management,
glad as I was of cracked slates
and a bolster for my head.

The tomb at Rodel

'Old Humpback'
with your fine broadsword
and your coat of mail –

so you survived another skirmish
west of Dunvegan. Was it you
slew the chieftain

of a rival clan?
All that trudging through bogs,
Alasdair Crotach,

rending the air
with a warrior's whoop
as you and your kinsmen

raced over the brae
for blood-letting
in the glen. Look at you

robed in black gneiss
and Carsaig stone
on the tomb the master mason

carved at your behest.
Satan and St. Michael
quibble over ounces,

while Clement holds
a crozier and a skull.
And you hunting stags

with your dogs and retinue,
or sat in a galley
trimming the sail.

Alexander MacLeod
of Skye and Harris,
angels may swing censers,

haloed apostles toil.
But Crotach you devil,
who did you love?

Date

for D.R., with apologies

Will you be dark or fair, short or tall,
as you come running towards me,
breathless, a smile breaking on your lips?
'Sorry to be late – the traffic was terrible!'
And we go bustling to a glad café, wanting
to know everything about each other.

I stood outside the station in this unknown
town – conspicuous blue rucksack,
blushing boy at the school dance. Had it
been wishful suggesting we meet when
I sensed your warmth on the phone, loved
your intonation, things you said?

All those years ago at my leaving do
I asked out the office secretary.
She was pretty, had a boyfriend –
I was fired with drink and pride.
Tuesday night, by Lewis's.
I thought again, and never went.

Passing Newcastle

I'll meet you under the lamp-post
by Gallowgate and Eldon Square.
Remember that concert at The Sage,
the music we couldn't hear?

Gorgeous cadences of Geordie
I'd never know in the corner shop;
shipping magnates' red brick towers
the day the clock on Guildhall stopped.

The city's mortar shared saliva –
in its smooth skin we'd be steeped.
Here where you came to feel at home
our sweat might mingle on the street.

I'd trace the tracks of Jarrow marchers,
steal through the cell of St. Bede...
The train draws out, a humdrum clatter –
next station Berwick-upon-Tweed.

Mr President

Kansas City, Kansas, 1967
or maybe Kansas City, Missouri –
I forget. A frail old man
with glasses and grey hair
came to the door,
held it ajar and waved.

Our posse leant on railings
fifty yards across the lawn.
They must have tipped him off
a scout troop from the old country
had hit town, and maybe
a greeting was appropriate.

There he was, no kidding –
Harry S., with whom
the buck stopped, in white shirt
and tie as I remember. And the hand
that had waved 'chocks away!'
to a plane that lifted west for Hiroshima.

Allende

Night was black in Puerto Montt.
Votes in the plebiscite had been counted –
the dictator's camp had won.
'What can I do?' The editor waved his arms,
picked out bold type for 'Yes to Pinochet'
as cars hooted 'I told you so' around the streets.

For three days I stayed in a *pensión*
run by a couple with a young child.
I walked by lakes, snow-capped volcanoes
where grass at least knew nothing of authority.
We got on well and warmed to one another,
but this was a time of 'general fear'.

On the third evening the man took down
a photo from the sideboard, showed me the family,
then slipped it from its frame. Behind
was a worn black and white snap
that he held up, smiling – like a locket,
silver buried in the garden.

The Honeymooners' Convention

One of those New York hotels of which Stalin would be proud
tapering fifty floors to a story-book sky
with lemon and flesh art deco hall, arresting but not loud.

We were in a room on the 17th, had drunk the mini-bar dry.
She almost wrestled me to the floor – only ten minutes to go
till the coffee break, but she said that was fine.

'When I packed my bag yesterday,' I confessed, 'you know
I took great care to include everything,
but it seems I left the condoms in a carrier by the phone.'

'Oh god.' She pulled up. 'Do you honestly think
I'm wearing this just to watch the news?'
'I hoped *you* might have brought some,' I mumbled. 'Your ring

looks so gorgeous – all ruby and diamonds.' 'It's sapphire blue,'
she snapped, standing up to dress. 'I'd thought this might be love.'
I wanted to say sorry, but was it... Sandra, Betty, Sue?

In the break I went to reception on the floor above
to ask discreetly if I could purchase... no one was there,
only men milling round in pinstriped suits looking suave

and smoking – so Edward fucking Hopper – I took the stairs
back down, was cold shouldered by my belle.
There was a spread of rich desserts, maybe apricots, pears –

the creamy toppings were so lavish it was hard to tell.
'Perhaps we'd better try them to find out,'
one woman suggested, and before long I was running hell

for leather to the 23rd, her kisses a shower
of maraschino cherries on my lips and neck.
She told me about Texas, her sorority and wedding vows,

that this was her seventh honeymoon but...what the heck,
she still felt like a virgin – I could only say
I wasn't a clairvoyant keeping fate in check

but hoped to meet my half orange one day.
She squeezed me, popped the buttons on my clothes
and ravished me like a spice king from Cathay.

I clung on tightly to my new betrothed.
'Could it be for real?' she mused amid the sighs.
'But there's the plenary coming up, I guess we'll both

be going there – it's starting prompt at five
and who knows what can happen after that
with tips on avoiding pelvic bruising and chapped thighs?'

'I suppose it'll be more of the same,' I said, 'and flat
out until dinner: do you take this man, that woman to be...?
Only the partners change – we've got the language pat.'

My two weeks up, I checked out in mid-February
feeling I'd run the whole gamut of bump and grind.
The snow and people attired made me blink to see –
all I know is I'll be staying at the Algonquin next time.

The Sacred Breakfast

Faslane Peace Camp, August 2017

Muesli, blueberries, soya milk
five yards from the road
and traffic pounding.

Lacework of sun, woodsmoke,
an insect on the page,
the morning waking.

Raspberries in the hedgerow,
an oystercatcher's squeal,
razor wire billowing

mile upon mile,
cartwheel of knives.
Warheads slip beneath the sea.

A driver hoots,
our sooted kettle,
easy steps on the muddy path.

Honey

The way to the monastery
was long and uphill
on an island afternoon
bright with Aegean sun –

the day before I'd found
a scorpion on a tree
next to my tent,
annihilated it.

The monks gathered honey,
people said, and sold it
in earthen jars to those
who trudged the six miles there.

A breeze ruffled our shirts,
caressed white houses among trees,
your blond hair darkening with sweat
as your friend walked on ahead.

Meli – the bees all know
what's shared is what is real.
Was there a windmill with white sails
above a sloping village street?

We pooled our thoughts, some fears
of camping out alone.
You told of Hamburg, city of sailors, home
mapping out the voyage to come.

A questioning tone in your voice.
Confiding – parallels of lives
in foreign places
now our own.

Would the monks be bearded patriarchs
with Makarios pill-box hats
like the spectre by a white, domed shrine
perched on a cliff below?

Our weighted steps, reflective, hot
through undergrowth, leaves,
a secret turn in the path.
I felt your hand was close.

So *this* was *meli* –
not where a monk
clasped his rough hands
round a pot.

We went for
honey on the hills
but your friend waited by a bend
and we walked on.

In a Hebridean cemetery

We are just stones,
somewhere between boulder and pebble
lodged on a mound of grass,
a twist of ewe's wool on the rusting wire.

Some a slab blotched with black and yellow
or a wafered menhir split in a storm.
The marram grass has grown so high
some of us are hardly noticed.

Iris blades crowd in a ditch below
and on the white *tràigh* clear waves lap the sand.
Shadow of Husival across the kyle –
a wheatear rides the wind on sapphire sea.

We are the people of Scarp.
We hauled our boats up the shore,
fetched water at the well,
combed the beach for driftwood, and sang.

MacInnes, MacLennan and MacLeod
by runrig furrows and the purple hill
that rang with schoolhouse voices.
Our names kissed others' lips before we went.

The Chinese poet Su Dongpo

Old Su Dongpo lugs two bales of straw
balanced from a pole over his shoulder
across the rickety bridge above the stream
that brings a torrent down from mountain snows.

A weak sun is still low among reeds.
Two brown-breasted ducks are looking sidelong
from their half-sleep plump on the lagoon
at bald Su, grey hairs tousled by breeze.

He trudges in leather sandals with a steady step,
dawn dweller, scythe tucked in his belt.
He'll walk pale green hillocks busy with leaves –
is his load thatch for a hut, fodder for hens? –

thoughts mirrored white and blue in still water
and I, Katsushika Hokusai, will paint his song.

Aurelio

I was on my way to do military service,
sitting on a bus with my twenty summers
reading magazines – nothing dirty:
you couldn't get that in Franco's day.
There was a cascade of glass,
the chassis buckled. I was trapped
between the seat in front and a lorry
peering in where the window had been.

I came to in hospital, groggy but alive,
my parents standing by the bedside.
I wanted to get up, but my mother
laid a hand on my shoulder. Do you know
what pleasure it gives me drawing on
a cigarette? That alone hauled me
from despair – my friend slipped me
a pack across the bed. The nurse saw me smile.

A person should be useful. My new leg fitted,
I ran a greengrocer's in Barbastro, served
customers for years. I got fed up with people
fingering the fruit, tossing aside
bruised apples, tomatoes a little soft.
We came back here – Luis, the teacher,
is a paying guest. The house was my grandparents' –
this heavy oak door's the same as then.

I can't walk over the hills to the *puente romano*
and see its arc etched in the river –
but how I savour a *mosto* in the village bar.
My handicap's landed me a job in Fraga
selling tickets in the lottery for the blind.
The kids are at school – Carmen's coming with me.
It isn't any woman, undressing at night,
who'd make love to a man with only one thigh.